KT-133-063

BLUFF YOUR WAY IN JAPAN

ROBERT AINSLEY

ℛℛ
RAVETTE BOOKS

Published by Ravette Books Limited
3 Glenside Estate, Star Road,
Partridge Green, Horsham,
Sussex RH13 8RA
(0403) 710392

Copyright© The Bluffer's Guides 1988
All rights reserved, including the right
of reproduction in whole or in part
in any form.

Series Editor – Anne Tauté

Cover design – Jim Wire.
Typesetting – System Graphics Ltd.
Printing & Binding – Cox & Wyman Ltd.
Production – Oval Projects Ltd.

The Bluffer's Guides are based on
an original idea by Peter Wolfe.

CONTENTS

INTRODUCTION

Japan is a daunting place for the business tripper or visitor. Its culture and customs are probably the most distinctive and complex in the world, which makes life there very difficult.

As this difficulty mainly affects the Japanese, you don't have to worry about it. They expect foreigners to know nothing at all about their country (usually with good reason), but will have enormous respect for you if you know, or at least appear to know, a little. They admire someone who has successfully done their homework because, in their insanely high-pressure education system, it's something few of them managed at school.

Everything is predictable and systematic in Japan (the air-conditioning season, for example, always starts on June 1. Even if it's ninety degrees in the shade on May 30th, nobody turns them on yet.) So, by reading this book, you can convince even Westerners who've lived there twenty years that you're well-travelled and extremely knowledgeable in all things Japanese, and your bluffs cannot be disproved.

Rather than talk about what Japan has – bullet trains, Mount Fuji, politeness – talk about what it hasn't. This gives the air of a true connoisseur.

Japan has no:

- geishas (any more, except in Kyoto)
- cheques (everything is done by cash or banker's draft
- flush lavatories (outside cities)
- word for 'filling' (in the dental sense)
- pierced ears (at all).

When dealing with Japanese, being an enthusiastic lover of their country and culture goes down very well, and will earn you lots of free nights out and make you very popular. The generosity and open-mindedness of the

Japanese will amaze and delight you (unless, of course, you're there to do business with them).

Japanese businessmen (they are all men; if you claim to have met a Japanese businesswoman people will know you are bluffing) drink every evening as a release from the pressure of work and moral codes of conduct. This, then, is the only time when they believe what each other says, because they know they're not just being polite, as they are the rest of the time. They never know whether to believe Westerners if you're drinking or not, but if you join in, at least you'll be having a good time.

In Japan never admit to having close Japanese friends. 'Business acquaintances' are the right sort of level and should be referred to as 'co-workers'.

Appearing the hapless foreigner, knowing not a word of Japanese, not being able to read station names, washing your hair in the o-furo and blowing your nose on restaurant napkins, pleases your hosts and reassures them that they can spend many hours patiently explaining Japanese customs, something they love doing and practise all the time in English lessons. They would get very worried by the prospect of having to talk about trade tariffs, discrimination by the Japanese against the Koreans, World War II and other things like that. So would you.

Bluffers therefore find themselves in the unusual position of faking a lack of knowledge of customs and language when dealing with the Japanese, while secretly knowing enough to use when it suits them. As the Japanese have not yet got around to inventing bluffing (along with strikes, cynicism and the letter 'l'), so long as you know what it is you're not supposed to know, (i.e. almost everything) you should easily be able to convince them of your ignorance.

THE COUNTRY

Japanese identify strongly with the island they come from, so know a little about each. The main islands are:

1. **Honshu**. The biggest island; some of it is Mount Fuji, some Tokyo, and the rest is the suburbs of Tokyo. If you meet a Japanese and they tell you where they live, you can say "That's just outside Tokyo, isn't it?" and never be far wrong. All the important things – chemical factories, highways, overcrowding, pollution – are in Honshu.

2. **Hokkaido**. Know that this means 'road to the north sea' but that it is further south than Rome. Japan's dairy products come from there because it's the only place where there's room for the cows, so on the rare occasions when you see milk, ask if it comes from Hokkaido and impress everyone with your knowledge of the country's agricultural infrastructure.

3. **Shikoku**. You can keep any group of Japanese busy for hours by asking "Is Shikoku famous for anything?"

4. **Kyushu**. The southernmost island. Despite the fact that there are demonstrably only four large islands in the archipelago, 'Kyushu' means 'ninth island'. Make up some outrageous theory to account for this. Kyushu is famous for its sweet tangerines; the word 'satsuma' is the old Japanese name for that province, so look your host straight in the eye and say solemnly "The English word for this is satsuma". It should confuse them, particularly as they call them 'mikan.'

There are 120 million Japanese, only about half of whom will come up to you in the street during your visit and ask you what you think about Japan. You can get into some good discussions about whether or not Japan is the most densely populated country in the world; Belgium and Holland have more people per square inch, but Japan

7

is more densely populated if you work on *inhabitable* land area. Five-sixths of Japan is uninhabitable because it is too mountainous; there are no roads, houses or factories, only pine trees. The remaining one-sixth, mostly on the coast, is uninhabitable because there is nothing but roads, houses and factories.

Houses

Never believe the famous misconception that Japanese houses are like rabbit-hutches. There are many things not possible in Japanese houses that are commonplace in rabbit-hutches; if not, there wouldn't be such a boom in 'love hotels' which rent out rooms by the hour. Houses are still based on wood and unlike Western houses which are built from 'the bottom up' they are built (you say) "from the top down – because of earthquakes".

Less than half of all toilets in Japan are flush types – the rest go down into cesspits which are emptied every few weeks by professional companies. You can speculate on the destination of this waste as you like.

Houses never have an address, only a postcode. This means it is impossible to find your friends' house when you go to see them and so every district has a 'kohban' or police box where they have maps and directories of everyone in the area and will tell you how to get there. Unfortunately no-one can ever find their way to the police boxes. If anyone asks you where a house is, say it is:

a) near that little shop with the coke and cigarette vending machines outside
b) not far from the main road
c) just round the corner from that little temple whose name you can't remember offhand

and you will always be right.

Volcanoes and Earthquakes

Japan has hundreds of active and dormant volcanoes. They are important. You only need know about two:

1. **Mount Fuji**, all 3776 metres of it (it always impresses people when you remember that) is the obvious one, and the only thing to know about it is the proverb which says anyone who doesn't climb Mount Fuji at least once in their life is mad, and anyone who climbs it more than once is mad too. You can have some interesting conversations about whether the summit has the highest vending machines in the world. Fuji is extinct now, but a definitely active volcano is:

2. **Sakurajima**, at the southern end of Kyushu. It erupts almost daily and people really do carry umbrellas even on fine days, to keep the ash off them. Remember that sakurajima means 'cherry tree island' and that its slopes are full of sweet tangerines not cherries, and it's on the mainland.

The volcanic nature of Japan's geology and its position on the edge of the Pacific plate make it very earthquake prone. If you are ever in one, never show fright; the Japanese just ignore them. They're ten a penny; there are hundreds a day somewhere in the country. If you tell a how-scared-I-was-in-last-night's-'quake story, they will listen attentively, laugh heartily, and change the subject. Things to remember about earthquakes are that:

a) the Japanese use their own scale to measure 'quakes, possibly because it makes them sound worse, or because no-one can pronounce 'Richter' properly;

b) the safest place to be in one is said to be in the w.c.;

c) Ireland is the most earthquake-free place in world, with no recorded occurrences;

d) the word for earthquake is 'jishin' which also means 'self confidence'.

THE PEOPLE

The image of the bespectacled Japanese businessman in the blue suit is not far wrong. Practically all Japanese wear spectacles and spend a great deal of their time asking each other their eye strengths. They know these figures to four decimal places so you must find out yours before you go. If in doubt say twenty-twenty; this reinforces their feelings of physical inadequacy towards Westerners. In Japan you need never worry about being caught out if your eyes are imperfect through not being able to tell people apart or not being able to read notices.

The very word for 'suit' in Japanese – sebiro – is a corruption of 'Savile Row', and the term inspires great respect. Always say your suit came from Savile Row, even if it was from the Savile Row Oxfam shop in Kingston-upon-Hull.

Japanese look younger than they are to Westerners, and love to play age guessing games. Always guess wildly low, of course, to please them, but you can tell their genuine ages quite easily by assessing their height. Height over 5′ is directly proportional to the percentage of hamburgers and instant noodles in the diet:

- 4′10″-5′4″ : 50 or over
- 5′4″-5′8″ : 30 to 50
- 5′8″-5′10″ : 20 to 30
- 5′10″-6′0″ : under 20
- 6′0″- : under 16

Japanese faces are like the Chinese characters they write with; you can see the differences once you know a few of them, but to the outsider they all look exactly the same and five minutes after seeing one you can't remember what it looked like. Certainly there is nowhere near the range in facial types you get in the West (though they can tell each other apart very easily and conversely often get Westerners confused – in fact Westerners in Japan spend much of their time being confused).

You should deny this and insist that there are actually hundreds of ways in which the Japanese are just as physically varied as Westerners. True, they are all dark brown eyed and black haired, but claim that there is a staggering range of features – narrow eyes, round eyes, long thin noses, flat noses, brown skin in the south to white skin in the north. This gives the appearance of acclimatisation and familiarity.

Whenever anyone mentions 'hair', you must mention the Ainu, a sort of Japanese Aborigine race, who have now been absorbed into mainstream society. They lived in the northern islands and must be referred to as "one of the hairiest people in the world". Point out if you like that this is a wild exaggeration based on the fact that, contrary to Asians in general, they actually can grow a moustache and beard without having to be 90 years old first.

Japanese History

The main recurring point throughout Japanese history is the ability to take other people's ideas and improve them. Japan's 'Westernisation' is only the most recent example of this; you should state that over the years the Japanese have adopted:

a)   agriculture and metal working from Korea (around the time of Christ)

b)   knowledge, writing and technology from China (4th century onwards)

c)   German army methods, English nautical knowhow, American education system (1900s)

d)   American influenced mass-culture (since the 1960s).

All you need to remember about Japanese history is this.

1250s: The Mongols came to invade Kyushu but an unexpected storm sank their fleet. This was called the

11

'kamikaze' or 'divine wind' and was later applied to suicide pilots.

1603: The capital moved from Kyoto to Edo, now Tokyo. Tokugawa Ieyasu made himself Shogun and the country was closed off for 250 years – the only Westerners allowed in were a small group of Dutch traders in Nagasaki. Society was preserved in a strict class system and the arts flourished.

1868: From being illegal, Western culture became compulsory overnight with the fall of the Shogunate. Japan westernised so quickly that within a few years it had electricity, trams, a constitution, etc.

Japan played in a few wars, beat the Russians in 1905 and lost to the Americans in 1945 with the dropping of the atom bombs over Hiroshima and Nagasaki. You should know that even more carnage was caused by normal incendiary bombing in the war, including 100,000 in one night in Tokyo.

Japan hit its lowest low after the war – the country was penniless and starving – and its comeback has been a miracle. Most middle-aged Japanese can remember having only a few grains of rice to eat a day.

The Emperor was regarded as 'divine' ("though not in our sense of the word", you should declare, implying you can see through some great Western misconception) in prewar Shinto, which was embraced as a militaristic national religion before the liberation of China, Taiwan and Korea. However, when the Americans liberated Japan in 1945 they made the Emperor renounce his divinity on live radio. The first line of his speech is worth remembering: Nagasaki and Hiroshima had fallen just a few hours before, and he said 'The war situation has not necessarily developed to our advantage.'

The whole business of the war is so depressing that no-one really wants to talk about it, so you can change the subject from history to something more cheerful and avoid having to know any of it.

12

TRAVEL

The Japanese 'Bullet Train' – the Shinkansen – is possibly the most famous train in the world. It's fashionable now to call it overrated, noting that:

a)   it is so expensive that flying most routes is cheaper and quicker

b)   the French TGV is much faster

c)   the British 125s are not much slower, are certainly cheaper and stop at more places than the Shinkansen – most of them stations.

Completed just before the Tokyo Olympics in 1964, it has been running 150mph services every twenty minutes since then, and the line now stretches from Kyushu to the far north of the mainland (or "right across the suburbs of Tokyo" if you like).

Things to do on a Shinkansen are:

a)   make a phone call from the in-car kiosks. Better, arrange for a friend to call you on the train; you can make everyone think you're the chairman of a multinational as you're summoned to your call and stride up the aisle muttering "Not Nomura on the phone again".

b)   buy 'o-miyage' (the obligatory souvenirs for everyone you know at home) from any town in Japan on the Shinkansen. So, if you didn't have time on your business trip to Kyushu to pick up some presents for your acquaintances, you can get sweets from Hakata, biscuits from Okayama and noodles from Osaka all from the hostess's trolley. Assume this is where anyone who travelled by train bought their souvenirs.

As well as the now-privatised Japan National Railways, there are dozens of smaller regional private railways. Many of them own large department stores placed handily next to the big stations, the most famous of

13

which is probably the Osaka firm of Hankyu. Point out that it has its nameplate designed to look suspiciously like 'Harrods'. Taking further inspiration from the West, Hankyu have strikes, regular as clockwork, every spring pay round. This is highly unusual in Japan but they strike in a very Japanese way. Make up stories about being delayed four minutes because of this annual go-slow for an hour at three o'clock in the morning.

Even on the smallest private railways you should never bother reading the timetable; although there are plenty at the station, trains in Japan are very frequent and never late. You just turn up knowing that you won't have to wait for more than ten minutes at the most.

Stations sell nearly all their tickets from machines, so if you don't happen to read Japanese, you won't be able to buy a ticket without asking for help. Luckily, place names are so difficult to read in Japanese that often the only people who will know the characters, or 'kanji', for the place you're going will be the locals, and even Japanese from outside the area would have to get assistance.

Every station has a constant stream of recorded announcements in Japanese. They are all very clear and well-spoken, so you can't pretend you didn't catch what they said because it was incomprehensible, as in British train announcements. However, even without under-standing a word you can convince anyone that you do. It is easy to bluff, because they are in three types.
1. Ones with music are advertisements for wedding halls or cram schools.
2. Ones without music are general announcements; if you must 'translate' to show your understanding of the language, choose from thank you for your honourable custom, be nice to old and disabled people, please don't try to board a train which is full, please be careful not to get on the wrong train, and the express is coming through and it doesn't stop here, please don't try to board it.

3.   Ones with a short jingle are train announcements.

Japanese trains are so infrequently late that on a delayed morning service the rail company issues a small certificate for each passenger to take to work confirming that the train was indeed late and that blame lies entirely with the railway company. Claim to have seen one; they are very rare and this would impress.

Commuter trains in Japan are jam-packed full of men in bluish suits and spectacles. Things to watch for and tell stories about are:

a)   occasions when they're so tightly squeezed that no-one can move their arms, and in winter, everyone's glasses steam up when they get inside, but they can't work their arms free to wipe them, so they're completely blinded and have to keep asking each other which station they've come to.

b)   how the porters really do push people on board the trains to make sure they're running nicely full.

c)   how it is a splendid demonstration of the way Japanese can work as one on a packed train; at any given moment, half the people are breathing in and half the people are breathing out.

d)   how Japanese commuters have the worst manners in the world; despite their extreme politeness to anyone they meet, on a train it's everyone for themselves. The pattern is to push and shove your way on to or off the train and blow anyone else.

Buses

The buses have even more persistent tape recorded announcements and advertisements on board. Throughout the journey passengers are treated to an unceasing commentary. If you are travelling with a Western friend, give the following as a 'translation' of it and you will always be about right:

'The next stop is the Hospital, which is also handy for Fukuda's Contact Lens Centre. After that the next stop will be the station. Thank you for your honourable custom. Please be nice to old people. Next stop, the hospital, and those wishing to visit Yamamoto's Ear Clinic should honourably alight here. Please be considerate to disabled people. Please mind the doors. Please do not bump your head as you get up. The bus has air brakes and the driver may find it necessary to humbly stop the bus abruptly, so we entreat your esteemed caution. Hospital, this is the hospital. Next stop is the Station, which is convenient for the Gynaecologist's. Thank you for your honourable custom . . .'

Never travel by bus for more than twenty minutes at a stretch.

Cars

It costs around two month's wages to get a driving licence in Japan – to pass the rigorous written and practical tests without the expensive Government-approved course is virtually impossible. Driving instruction is all done on special courses; it is thought too dangerous to let novices out on to the road. Tell everyone they should fly to England or the States to get their licence – they'd get a free holiday and it would still work out cheaper. (Preferably England, as they also drive on the left.)

Bluffers know things that only people who've really experienced the country would know:

a)   no-one in Japan ever changes down to go round a corner – they pull away in top having left the bend at twenty miles an hour

b)   all the cars are white. You can pass yourself off as a psychic by guessing that the businessman about to buy you a drink in amazement drives a white Toyota

c)   all cars are brand new. You never, ever see an old car

16

on the road and second-hand cars lose their value
very quickly in Japan.

d) a modification required by law in Japan makes the
speedometer emit an unstoppable and continuous
dink-donk whenever the car is travelling at more
than the 100km/h speed limit

e) demonstrably green traffic lights are called 'blue' in
Japan.

Planes

Generally avoided by bluffers, since it is like flying
anywhere. Like everything else in Japan they're expensive and highly organised. The main airline JAL is still
trying to get over the legal fall-out from the crash in 1985
which killed 520 people – they had only just finished the
court-case aftermath of a previous crash which was
caused by a schizophrenic pilot who thought he was a
kamikaze fighter and crash-landed a domestic flight into
the harbour by Haneda airport shortly after take off.

Trams

Only someone who's really been to Japan would know
how widespread trams are, so they're good things to talk
about. Many towns in the west (Kagoshima, Nagasaki,
Hiroshima to name three) have them. The original trams
and lines are still operational from pre-war days, still very
cheap and cheerful and clanking a lot.

Hotels

The traditional Japanese style of hotel is the ryokan.
Don't bother trying to say this word as it is extraordinarily difficult to do properly; it has three syllables of
equal spoken length, ryo, ka, and n. Just laugh at
Westerners when they say it.

In the ryokan you have a traditional Japanese style room complete with tatami (straw mats) on the floor, wood-and-paper shoji (sliding screens), futon (mattresses), a low heated kotatsu (table), and a terebijon setto (TV set). Outside there will be a little garden to soothe the senses, and as you sit after your o-furo (bath) wearing your yukata (dressing gown) drinking your sake (sake), you will wish you had a Japanese dictionary.

The classic mistake made by foreigners is thinking that the bath is for washing. A Japanese bath is a hot tub for soaking, and you wash yourself down with bowls of water before getting in. Offer as proof of your acclimatisation, the fact that you can't understand how Westerners can happily sit in a bath full of dirty water.

Remember that the screens between the rooms are paper-thin, because they're made of paper. Thus you can hear everything that's going on in the next room, and vice versa. And you can probably see quite a bit too.

Always tell anyone staying at a ryokan that it's a waste of money – they really are extremely expensive. Tell them they should have stayed at a minshuku, a small family-run 'hotel' which provides the traditional food and Japanese-style room, at half the price.

Tell anyone staying at a minshuku that they're getting the worst of both worlds – still sleeping on the floor and eating rice, fish and raw eggs for breakfast, lunch and dinner, but not getting the class and elegance of a ryokan, which might have its own hot springs. Stay at a minshuku once, but unless you have a lot of money or particularly like raw eggs for breakfast, go for a standard Western style hotel. This is far more 'traditionally Japanese' now than the ryokan or minshuku.

The cheapest hotels are called Bijinesu Hoteru or 'Business Hotels'. For a few thousand yen you get the basic essentials a Japanese businessmen needs on his overnight stop: a bed, a shower, a clean room, a beer and cup-noodle vending machine and a stock of pornographic videos on the television. Tell anybody staying at a hotel that they're mad; they can stay at a hotel at home. They should be experiencing traditional Japan in a minshuku or ryokan.

There are also 'capsule hotels', miniature boxes stacked in rows near stations where businessmen who have missed the last train home or can't get in to the proper hotels can stay the night in a box complete with miniature TV, miniature hand basin and 8mm porn videos. Insist that capsule hotels are overrated; they are only places to use in an emergency.

Sightseeing

Everything in Japan is listed and documented, and when talking about where you went, describe it as "the 15th most scenic spot in the prefecture" or "one of the twenty-nine famous sights in that part of Japan".

At the very top of the list are the Big Three: Amanohashidate, Miyajima, and Matsushima. These are the three sights in Japan renowned for being of outstanding natural famousness.

Amanohashidate. You must claim to have been here. It is on the northern seabord, somewhere in the recesses of rural Kyoto prefecture. It is a small bay whose entrance is almost closed off by a long sand bar covered with pine trees. If you climb the nearby hill, stand on the viewing platform, bend over with your head between your legs and look backwards, you will be looking at one of the most famous sights there is. The name comes from the fact that with this new inverted perspective the sand bar looks like a bridge into the skies. You know better, of course, it looks like a long sand bar covered with pine trees seen upside down.

Explain enthusiastically how people come from all over

Japan to see this spectacle – of perfectly sensible people bent over looking underneath their legs.

Miyajima. A shrine near Hiroshima built on stilts so that, at high tide, it appears to be floating on a shimmering sea. The 'torii', or entrance gateway, is out in the sea. The shrine is on an island which makes it easy for you to remember confidently that 'miya' means 'shrine' and 'jima' means 'island'.

Matsushima. Matsushima is a collection of islands now rather heavily touristed in a bay near Sendai in the north-east, recognised as the most beautiful place in Japan. Unfortunately this was over a hundred years ago. Lament the industrial development.

A good obscure sight to claim to have seen is the centuries-old cormorant fishing which takes place on the river Kiso and elsewhere in central Japan. Only a true connoisseur would know about it. The activity itself is rather dull – a bird-keeper dressed in traditional clothes pilots a boat with several trained cormorants on string leashes. The cormorants are trained to catch delicious ayu – sweetfish – which rise to the surface attracted by the bundle of burning straw waved over the prow by some assistants. When the birds bite, the cormorant-master pulls the birds in tightly by the leash, which half-strangles them and enables him to prise the fish out. The thing to talk about is not the catching of the fish but the fact that it is then served on the tables of the restaurant boat behind, full of spectators who've paid fifty quid for the privilege of eating regurgitated fish.

The best reason for talking about cormorant fishing is that the word for cormorant in Japanese is the single vowel u, spoken very abruptly and in a rather high pitch, rather like the noise Westerners make when trying to talk to chimpanzees. Japanese being the economical language it is, a one word answer is usually deemed sufficient to any question, so that if you ask "How do you say cormorant in Japanese?", somebody will answer u. Ask again and they'll repeat, u. Look puzzled, and ask a third time, and everyone will join in, saying u,u,u,u,u. You can reduce a group of respectable, intelligent, middle-class businessmen to a group of gibbering primates in thirty seconds.

Other words you can try this with are 'picture' (e) and 'stomach' (i).

General Sightseeing

You can be dismissive about the best known sights or tourist destinations deliberately. Describe the hundreds of coke/beer/cigarette vending machines, the endless crocodiles of school children out on trips, the American tourists, the Japanese tourists, the horrible local rice dumplings called 'dan-go' sold in ugly little stalls. Even those who live there will be convinced.

Instead you should enthuse most about the *local* sights you saw in the countryside where you stayed. Mention:

a)   that lovely out-of-they-way shrine called something-something-jingu on the side of the hill near where you stayed

b)   that newly-built-at-great-expense temple called something-something-ji at the top of a hill near where you lived, only accessible via a four-mile mountain footpath, and a tarmac road for coach parties

c)   the villagers who kept inviting you in for Japanese tea and cakes, lending you umbrellas and giving you lifts to places where people had never met foreigners before

and you'll always sound plausible.

LEISURE

Knowing what the Japanese do with their spare time is vital if you are to bluff intimate knowledge of the people. Fortunately the answer is very easy: most Japanese don't have any spare time. What little time they don't spend at work they spend 'sleeping' or 'watching television'.

Men don't have any spare time. Golf is hallowed in Japan and incredibly expensive; it is not a leisure activity – it is always linked with work. Membership of a club can cost as much as a car; rounds cost up to any price so you can make figures up and they'll be believable. Memberships can be sold just like real estate so "they're more of an investment". Point out how cheap golf is in Britain.

For most Japanese golf means the local driving range. This will be a huge floodlit box of netting on the outskirts of the town. As visitors to Japan are always mystified by this you must be able to identify your local range.

Women are allowed to have free time in Japan but are only allowed to spend it preparing for marriage by:

a) playing tennis
b) studying the tea ceremony
c) going to cookery classes
d) learning something arty (the koto, ikebana etc.).

The most Japanese of sports is sumo wrestling. The pre-fight ritual is elaborate and involves a lot of standing on one leg with the other raised in the air – ("to show that no dangerous weapons are being carried", you can say quite truthfully). The fighting itself is between two enormous Japanese who lock each other in a hold. The first one to fall over, step outside the ring or lose weight is beaten. The most popular wrestlers are never the best, but the fattest. Current heaviest are Onokuni and Konishiki, the latter being the only recently successful foreigner in sumo – a Hawaiian and Samoan (at the same time) who plays American football and the trumpet (not at the same time) and weighs nearly forty stone.

The only thing to remember about sumo wrestling is that the larger wrestlers are so fat they cannot wipe their own behinds, and have special assistants, who are young sumo apprentices, to do it for them. You cannot translate 'starting at the bottom' into Japanese or even explain it in English, so don't try. They are also reputed to be able to withdraw their testicles inside their bodies to prevent damage. You can either claim this is truth or fallacy but may as well note that most of them are so fat no-one can tell.

There are many ways of winning a bout, but unless one of the wrestlers has just fallen over, the win was probably by 'yorikiri' (stepping outside the ring) so you can say "That was yorikiri, wasn't it?" and sound intelligent and knowledgeable about the sport.

Gateball is a good source of jokes. It's a form of croquet played exclusively by retired people in municipal parks at five thirty in the morning, a sort of Japanese bowls, and asking anyone under 50 if they play gateball is guaranteed to get everyone falling about laughing.

Most Westerners will have heard of mah-jongg (correct their pronunciation to the Japanese version 'maa-jan'). It is played with tiles, not cards. If you get into a game the thing to do is keep taking sharp intakes of breath through your teeth, saying "warui no kita naaa" (that was a bad tile) and looking thoughtful. Because it is a finely balanced game of skill and fortune you can blame bad luck when you lose and credit your skill when you win. The winner is the one last left able to see the tiles after the quantities of sake drunk. Its purpose is, you say, a way for four businessmen to spend an evening drinking, having a great time and not having to say anything to each other.

Good bluffing ground is the amazingly popular pachinko parlour. Pachinko is a sort of vertical bagatelle machine ("invented after the war by a ball bearing manufacturer who had a surplus load of balls" you can say quite truthfully). Pachinko halls are huge arcades lined with machines stretching as far as the eye can see. No-one knows how big they really are because they fill with cigarette smoke before they can be measured. They resound with the infernal clatter of a million balls plinking around the game consoles. They are not difficult to spot; every high street has one.

Don't bother playing pachinko as it is dreary and a waste of money. You enter, buy a certain amount of balls, feed them into the machine, turn a knob to regulate the speed of entry, and get more balls released if any of the bearings find their way (quite at random) into certain holes.

The most important and exciting bit to talk about at length is at the end. It's illegal to win money at Pachinko, so the balls can be exchanged not for cash but for gifts – usually the same gift, for example a set of very useful pipe cleaners for every hundred balls. But, just round the corner, behind the pachinko hall, down the alley and next to the pawnshop, there'll be a little hole in the wall where you can exchange your nineteen new and unopened packets of pipe cleaners for cash. The police turn a blind eye to it, but you should tell of how you sneaked down the alley, talking in French to confuse the cops, took the money with your back to the window and pretending to look in the opposite direction while reading a paper with two holes in it to watch through, and generally acted like a KGB agent in a Bond film.

If someone else tells you this story, say all their subterfuge is quite unnecessary – you know for a fact that all the police in that part of Japan are in the pockets of the local gangsters, and most of them were probably inside the hall playing anyway, and the ones that get thrown out for non-enforcement of the law just start up pipe cleaner factories.

CULTURE

Culture is vigorously preserved in Japan. It is either violent and brutal and done exclusively by men (martial arts) or calm, meditative and artistic and done exclusively by women (music, flower arranging, tea ceremony, calligraphy, etc.). However, women are allowed to *learn* but men can only be *masters*.

Martial Arts

Judo was invented by a Tokyo university graduate called Kano in 1882 and means 'way of gentleness'. It is supposed to be a non-aggressive art and the Japanese are at pains to point out that you need neither strength nor bulk to succeed, a point you should counter by declaring that the recent world champion Yamashita was 6'5″ and weighed twenty stone. If a Westerner mentions 'black belt', point out that a black belt is not the highest attainable. Those who have attained the top grade, or tenth dan, wear a belt of colour 'koh' ("difficult to translate in English", you say, "as it is the colour they call brown tea-leaves, crimson sunsets and bright red autumn foliage").

Karate is often quoted as meaning 'empty hand' so you can sound authoritative by noting that the 'kara' bit actually comes from the region of China where it originated and just happens to sound the same as the word for 'empty'. The locals in Okinawa developed it after weapons had been banned there and if you meet someone who does it, never mention anything about breaking piles of slates with your head.

Kendo is 'the way of the sword' and involves two men wearing face masks and skirts smashing each other over the head with bamboo sticks. If you see a young man walking along the road wearing a skirt and carrying a bamboo stick, this is probably what he has been doing (unless you're in certain sections of Tokyo at night). Kendo is great for competitions. **Aikido** is a more spiritual, purely defensive martial art, and is therefore a less suitable basis for competitions, at least ones with winners.

Non-martial Arts

Calligraphy (**shodoh**) is one of the most venerated and respected of all art forms. Good calligraphers make the Chinese characters almost into abstract pictures, and experts can make even a well-known poem totally illegible. If you go to a calligraphy display, don't claim you can read any of the exhibits. Stare contemplatively and say what the Japanese themselves would say: "I can't read it, but I can understand such a feeling."

Ikebana is flower arranging and the only thing you need remember is that there is more than one accepted school of arrangement style – perhaps three thousand in fact. You can make up any Japanese sounding word, ask if the arrangement in your host's house is that school, and gain cudos, because there's bound to be a school of that name somewhere. A good genuine one to remember is 'nage-ire' where flowers are literally thrown into a vase and arrange themselves.

Paper folding, or **origami**, is well known in the West. The only thing to know is that when someone is ill, the Japanese often give a get-well present of 1,000 paper cranes (a crane lives 1,000 years according to legend). It always works, because it takes so long to make that if in the meantime the invalid hasn't died they must be on the way to recovery.

Probably the most famous of the Japanese traditional arts is the tea ceremony. This is a special ceremony, its origins in Zen meditation, consisting of a few people

26

sitting uncomfortably on their legs for an hour while drinking powdered green tea indistingishable from poster paint, except that the poster paint possibly tastes better. Things to do in a tea ceremony are:

a) say it's your first beforehand – then everyone will be very enthusiastic and helpful, tell you what to do, excuse your spitting out the tea, and so on
b) claim not to be able to sit 'properly' with your legs tucked underneath you – you'll be encouraged to sit as normal, cross-legged, which will please not only you but all the Japanese men there who can also assume a comfortable sitting posture and not be the first to have cracked
c) appreciate the cup after you drink out of it by looking at the design on the bottom and spinning out a thoughtful "hoooohhhhh . . ." to yourself (you don't have to say anything sensible, just look contemplative).
d) do not say anything during the ceremony, wait what to be told to do, and if you want to really impress them when they ask you if you enjoyed it, appear to struggle personfully before saying, laboriously, "kekko desu" (it is excellent).

Art

Japanese art is a good area to display knowledge – those prints of women in kimonos and landscapes with Mount Fuji in the background which can be found everywhere. If you can identify the artist, which does not need any detailed knowledge or interpretative skill, is much admired.

First claim that the only print artists worth knowing about are **Utamaro**, **Sharaku**, **Hokusai** and **Hiroshige**. Then decide which of these was responsible for the print as follows:

If there's deep blue in the picture, it must be post-1830s (Prussian blue did not arrive from China until then) which rules out the first two. If there's Mount Fuji in the picture somewhere, it's by Hokusai. If not, it's by Hiroshige.

If there's no deep blue in the picture, it will be by Utamaro if it features a beautiful woman in a kimono, and by Sharaku if it's a head-only caricature of a man (he specialised in actor portraiture) – but watch out for men dressed as women (female roles have traditionally been taken by men in Japanese theatre).

Point out that Utamaro and his contemporaries are the ones to blame for the Western perception of the Japanese as a narrow slanty-eyed race; in the highly conventionalised world of Japanese art, all women appeared with narrow eyes, when in reality the shape can be anything from linear to circular.

The most popular examples of the Japanese print in the West are Hokusai and Hiroshige's series of landscapes. These always came in sets, a little like cigarette cards, except that cigarettes had not yet arrived from the West in the mid-1800s. For example, Hiroshige produced the famous *53 Stations on the Tokaido* and *69 Stations on the Kisokaido*, a set of pictures dedicated to the 19th century Japanese equivalent of motorway services, except that motorway services had not yet arrived in the West in the mid-1800s.

Hokusai produced the most famous examples of Japanese art in the West, and should generally be your first guess. He did the rather abstract picture of Fuji in fine weather in which the mountain is depicted as bright red (point out its real colour is a volcanic grey). His series included *Thirty Six Views of Mount Fuji* (in which there were forty-six views) and *The Sea in a Thousand Pictures* (which consisted of ten).

Haiku

These inconclusive short poems always have the same
form: three lines in a pattern of 5-7-5 syllables. They
attempt to express a lot in a few words and so tend to start
on something mundane and generally seasonal (such as a
reference to cherry blossom falling or autumn leaves
turning brown or air conditioning being turned on), then
jump in the last line to eternal verities or cosmic
observations. A typical example is:

'Araumi ya	A rough sea and
Sado ni yokotau	Stretching over Sado
Amanogawa'	The Milky Way

(Amanogawa = heavenly river = Milky Way)

Haiku "always lose something in the translation" a fact
which is obvious even to someone who doesn't know a
word of Japanese, but which makes you sound clever if
you say it right. The above haiku was the work of Basho,
the most famous classical haiku writer. It was inspired by
the rugged northern coast off the island of Sado, and not
marijuana, which is unobtainable and extremely illegal
in Japan. The 5-7-5 pattern has deeply penetrated the
Japanese consciousness and being able to spot a sentence
of this pattern, even in the middle of a tax demand or
business contract, will impress no end.

Music

Japanese music was, until this century, based around the
koto (a horizontal thirteen-string harp with a characteristic plink-plonky sound) the **shamisen** (a three-string
banjo plucked with those things you use to scrape the ice
off windscreens with a characteristic plink-plonky sound)
and the **shakuhachi** (a keyless bamboo flute which is
almost impossible to get a note out of and has a

characteristic badly-played sound). Only women learn the koto and shamisen and only men learn the shakuhachi, though to compound things for a woman 'to play the shakuhachi' is a euphemism for oral sex in Japanese. Never therefore ask a woman if she plays the shakuhachi.

The only modern composer you need know about is Takemitsu ("Some interesting influences of the Japanese musical ethos on Western forms", that sort of thing).

Festivals and Holidays

Shatter everyone's conceptions of hard-working Japanese by noting that there are over a dozen public holidays a year in Japan. Then restore them by saying that nobody actually takes them.

Shogatsu: New Year
Point out solemnly that the Japanese New Year, oddly enough, is celebrated on January 1st. (Oddly, you say, because you might expect it to be in February, as is the Chinese festival.) The method of counting the years, however, is different. 1990, for example, will only be '65. Japan numbers years according to the reign of the Emperor: 1989 will be the sixty-fourth year of Hirohito (which as you should point out, ought to make it year number sixty-three. Such things do not bother the Japanese, who call his first year, year one, contrary to all known numerical logic, despite the fact that they are the best mathematicians in the world. Under this old system, babies were born at the age of one, and added on another year every January 1st. Hence a baby born on December 31st became two on January 1st, a day later, which may help to explain why twelve year-old Japanese have a mathematical age of fifteen).

The year in Japan is thus referred to as Showa 63, Showa 64, etc., Showa being the name of the current imperial era (that of Emperor Hirohito) and meaning 'peaceful enlightenment', a phrase coined in the militaristic and expansionist atmosphere of the late twenties.

Other good periods to know are:
a) Taisho (1912-1926) – the emperor was loopy
b) Meiji (1868-1912, when Japan suddenly hit on the idea of nicking ideas from the Westerners instead of refusing to talk to them at all)
c) Edo (1603-1868), the Shogun period.

The Japanese find it extraordinarily hard to convert to Western calendars and you can amuse yourself by testing them on the dates of The Great Tokyo Earthquake (1923); the Meiji Restoration (1868); and the opening of the Shinkansen bullet train service (1964).

Everyone spends the first hours of January 1st trying to work out which number year it actually is.

Adults' Day (January 15)
All those who have reached twenty years of age in the preceding year are deemed to be proper members of society, i.e. they can now smoke and drink. They all go along to their Town Hall dressed in their kimonos and designer suits and have speeches from the mayor on being a responsible member of society, the future is in your hands, we look to you to build a better tomorrow, and so forth. Don't be fooled; force the person telling you about their ceremony to admit that they all then went out, got extremely drunk and threw up on the last train home.

National Foundation Day (February 11), Vernal Equinox Day (February 21), Emperor's Birthday (April 29), Constitution Day (May 3)
There is no particular reason for these but at least you don't have to eat any special sticky rice things as you do on most other festival days.

The period over the end of April/beginning of May contains four public holidays and is called Golden Week. Don't make the mistake of thinking this is a good thing for the average Japanese family. This is the time when trains are traditionally packed; unfortunate people whose families live in Hokkaido but who work in Kyushu have to spend three days standing on a train travelling home and three days travelling back. Just keep sympathising with "taihen desu ne" (it's really bad, isn't it) when people tell you it's Golden Week.

Respect for the Aged Day (September 15), Autumnal Equinox Day (September 23), Sports Day (October 10th), Culture Day (November 3), Labour Thanksgiving Day (November 23)
Sports Day is celebrated by everyone sitting at home watching television or sleeping, Culture Day is the time for visiting the traditional burger bars down the road, and on Labour Thanksgiving Day, everyone celebrates the holiday by going to work.

There are a few well-loved and enthusiastically celebrated festivals which are not quite important enough to merit a day off work which nobody takes.

Setsubun (early February)
You throw beans around all evening and shout "Oni waaaaaaaa soto! Fuku waaaaaaa uchi!" (Devils out! Good fortune in!) at the top of your voice. Quite a few go to temples and do it over a sake or two. If asked why people do this, talk about the cleansing out of inner devils and bad spirits within, then give up and just admit it's all great fun.

Girls' Day (May 3); Boys' Day (May 5)
Although the holiday 'Children's Day' is on the 5th, the 3rd is really Girls' Day and the 5th Boy's Day. The boys hang up windsocks painted to look like carp to encourage them to grow tough and courageous. Always pretend that you think the carp is a really great fish because it struggles upstream to spawn and then die and agree that this is a splendid thing to aspire to (but only for a boy).

Girls (i.e. housewives) get out their doll collections and put them on show. Always look impressed by a doll display and say "They must have been very expensive", because they are. You must agree that having a doll collection is a really good thing to aspire to for a girl. You can sneakingly admit that you think the dolls are a symbol of male repression; if the housewife's husband hadn't spent his end-of-year bonus on the dolls, he'd have spent it in a hostess bar.

Cherry Blossom Festival
In April/May the cherry trees or 'sakura' blossom throughout Japan. 'Hanami' are viewing parties and consist of a blanket on the grass in a park somewhere under a tree with huge amounts of Japanese food and sake. The only thing you must talk about for the couple of weeks or so when the sakura is in blossom is what percentage of trees are in bloom. Have deep and considered discussions about whether it is currently fifty or sixty per cent in bloom.

Tanabata (July 7)
According to the ancient Chinese fairy tale, the Cowherd star is able to cross the Milky Way and meet his lover the Weaver star. He can see her only once a year, but is in no position to complain – like the Japanese businessmen who are posted away from home by their companies.

O-Bon (late July/early August)
The souls of the dead come back to earth and everyone in Japan returns to their ancestral home. This is the usual time for large firms' summer breaks, giving every worker the chance to spend their holiday on a train visiting their parents in Kyushu. In Kyoto huge fires are lit as a send-off to the spirits in the shape of the character for 'big', so when it's shown on television you can pretend to be able to read it and everyone will be impressed.

Shichi-go-san (November 15)

The ages three, five and seven, are 'unlucky' in Japanese folklore (though you don't need to know why, as nobody else does) and parents take children of these ages in their kimonos to temples to pray for good luck. So, if you see children in a kimono being taken to a temple by their parents on this day, you can amaze them by knowing how old their children are.

Other Festivals

If anyone wonders why there are so many festivals when the Japanese have such a hard-working image, point out that most of them are hard work.

There are countless festivals across the country during the year. The big ones are in Kyoto (called *Aoi Matsuri*, *Jidai Matsuri* and *Gion Matsuri*) and involve processions of townsfolk dressed in period costume and troupes of young men wearing gaudy jackets carrying portable shrines called mikoshi. Smaller scale ones can be found anywhere at almost any time. The smaller ones are in some ways much more interesting than the grand processions of Kyoto. Do not say:

a) "The people carrying the mikoshi look drunk" (they are)

b) "The mikoshi looks heavy" (the only way they can carry it is to get drunk first).

These festivals are usually accompanied by rows and rows of little streetside stalls selling everything from Mickey Mouse masks to more traditional, but less tasty, fried squid and octopus kebabs. If anyone asks what it is they're selling, "squid" or "octopus" is a good bet and few people will then buy and eat it to test your theory. You can safely assume anyone linked with the stalls is a 'yakuza', or gangster. Look for the tattoos and the perm.

The summer is the time for firework festivals – plenty of them. They last for hours and have the usual stalls. Every town claims to have the biggest in Japan. If you want to quibble say either Osaka's or Tokyo's is bigger, or if you want to sound really knowledgeable, try Okazaki or Inuyama.

There are also some imports from the West which are not public holidays:

Valentine's Day (February 14)
Two things to remember.
1. All the girls send their boyfriends chocolate. However, to be sure not to leave anyone out they also sent it to their bosses, brothers, English teachers, friends, next-door neighbours and next-door neighbour's brothers. Therefore men should never assume just because a girl has sent chocolate that she is in love with them. The only sure way of telling this is if the girl says nothing about marriage at all and invites them to see her parents.
2. The Japanese are perplexed at our custom of sending anonymous cards. How do you know who it's from, they ask, if there's no name on it? Say this is just another example of the Japanese being more logical than Westerners.

The boyfriends are supposed to send chocolate to the girls on 'White Day' one month later. They never do and neither should you.

Sundays
All the shops are open but all the bank cashpoints are closed. This is a good time to discuss the ridiculous Sunday trading laws in Britain, though it doesn't matter why you think they are ridiculous.

Don't get caught out by Sundays or public holidays: even on public holidays, all the shops are open in Japan, and all the trains run a Sunday service (frequent and punctual) unlike Britain where all the trains run as normal (erratically and late).

JAPANESE SOCIETY

You must profess an intimate knowledge of how Japanese society works. Everyone probably knows by now that the group ethic is the motivating force; all decisions in business or society tend to be taken with the good of the group as the ultimate aim, and once the consensus has been reached no-one will argue with it or complain about it. You should therefore take this as read and be dismissive about it.

Most decisions in a Japanese adult's life are really taken for him or her by a nebulous group of people starting with the parents and ending with everyone in the country. You should know how and by whom things are decided:

- the job is largely determined by the University, which is determined by the school, which is determined by the Junior school, etc.
- the marriage will probably be arranged by a friend of the family, or else school/college/workmates will decide for themselves
- important things (who to vote for, what the position on Article 9 of the Constitution should be, why trade sanctions should be imposed on South Africa) are decided by the husband
- minor things (what to spend money on, what school to send the kids to, what car to buy) are decided by the wife
- really trifling things (like where in Japan the family will live, how they'll spend their leisure time, when they'll be posted abroad) are decided by the company.

A Day in the Life ...

The best way to explain to others what it's like in Japan to be Japanese, is to describe the day of this family. They live in a small Japanese-cum-Western house on the outskirts of a small town, near the station, by the hospital, just off the main road, at the foot of a little group of hills, somewhere just outside Tokyo.

Mr. Ohta works as a 'sarariman' – a middle-class white-collar worker – in a biggish chemical company. Mrs. Ohta teaches English part-time and studies flower arranging. They have three children, a girl and two boys. The girl, Emi, is 21, a graduate of Kyoto (one of the top universities in Japan) and works as an office tea woman. The elder boy, Hiroshi, is 18, and has just failed the entrance exams to the local big university, so he is taking a year out to study at a cram school to re-take the exams next year. Takashi is 15 and goes to the local Junior High School.

Also in the house live Mrs. O's retired parents, Mr. and Mrs. Koizumi. This is not a typical Japanese family; it is every Japanese family.

0630
Everyone wakes up, except for Takashi who's been awake studying for his maths test today since five fifteen, and the women who've been up since six making the men's 'bento' or lunchboxes. Mr. and Mrs. K have rice and fish for breakfast. The kids have coffee and 'bread'. Mr. O has nothing because he has to rush for the 7.03 from the station down the road.

0700
The boys leave for their schools. Takashi is worried because he's lost a button from his black school uniform. This could have serious repercussions if any of the teachers notice, last time it happened he had to clean the entire school.

0715
Takashi, Hiroshi, Emi and Mr. Ohta are all asleep on their respective trains. Fortunately they each get off at big stations and get swept off by the rush.

37

0830
Mr. Ohta is hard at work already. The boys have arrived at school.

0900
Emi is at the employee's morning assembly in her office. The boss is telling everyone to work hard. Everyone agrees and bows low. Emi starts work and resolves to make the coffee and do the photocopies really well today.

0900-1230
Everyone's working straight through, no breaks. Mr. Ohta is sifting through some paperwork. The boys are looking out of the windows in lectures. Emi is making coffee and doing photocopies.

1230
Lunch. Everyone opens their bento lunchboxes. Mmm! Rice! What a surprise. Mr. Ohta carries on working through his lunch break as there's some paperwork to catch up on. Emi goes for a walk all the way round the local park.

1232
Emi finishes her walk.

1400
Meanwhile back at home Mrs. Ohta is round the corner having a lesson at her local flower arrangement teacher's. Mrs. Koizumi is preparing dinner; Mrs. O won't have time to do it tonight because she's teaching English at a cram school.

1530
The boys are busy doodling in some lectures. Mr. Ohta works through his break as he has some urgent paper-work to be photocopied.

1700
Takashi is in his compulsory hour of school tennis,

practising being a ballboy. Hiroshi is doing some prep. Emi is just finishing off the last lot of photocopies. It's time to go home.

1830
Well, not quite time. Mr. Ohta is staying behind to finish off some urgent paperwork. Emi is staying behind to make the coffee for the men doing overtime in her office. Takashi is on the train to his evening class in English. He reads a comic on the train. So do all the businessmen on their way home.

1900
Hiroshi and Emi are home and eating dinner – hamburger and rice. Mr. and Mrs. K are eating rice and fish. Takashi is busy shading in all the o's in the textbook in his English class. Mr. Ohta and his colleagues go out to a small restaurant to clear up some points arising from today's paperwork.

2030
Takashi arrives home and starts his homework for tomorrow's History exam. Hiroshi is watching television. Emi is getting ready to go out with her boyfriend. Mr. Ohta and his colleagues go on to a small karaoke bar to tie up a few loose ends arising from today's discussions.

2130
Emi arrives back home just in time for her nine thirty curfew.

2200
Mr. Ohta and his colleagues go on to a small hostess bar to go over one or two matters which may well arise in tomorrow's paperwork. Takashi starts his homework for next Thursday's Japanese exam.

2330
Mr. Ohta gets home, has some pickles and rice to sober up, and takes a bath.

0100
Everyone goes to bed except Takashi, who just has today's homework to do, and the women, who clear up after Mr. Ohta.

Overtime

It's true that the Japanese do a fantastic amount of overtime, generally an extra day a week and a couple of hours a night. Everyone knows this, but only the bluffer knows that the Japanese call it 'overwork' rather than 'overtime' due to a mistranslation.

However, point out that this overtime business is not all it seems to be; if you look into an office full of overtimers at one o'clock in the morning, they never actually seem to be doing anything. This is partly to keep up the appearance of dedication to duty, partly due to most Japanese houses being so small that they can't get into the house until everyone else is in bed.

Talk confidently about the real sweatshops, the ones the casual visitors and business trippers never see; the small businesses, tiny family-run factories you 'saw' which were at it sixteen hours a day.

Sooner or later someone will ask why the Japanese are successful. It is simple, you say: they work harder and better than anyone else and don't cause trouble. Make light of any other, more sophisticated 'explanations'. For example, someone might propose the following reasons why the Japanese are beating the Americans economically – your reply is in brackets:
a) superior business management methods (no: they copied those from the Americans)
b) advanced ideas on quality control (actually they got those from the Americans too)
c) the union systems which tie management and workers together in a non-militant way (the Americans created their unions system after the war)

d)   a superior education system (the Japanese modelled theirs on the American pattern).

Marriage

This is a very different proposition in Japan to that in the West – in fact the men very rarely propose at all. Although 'love marriages' are said to be on the increase, many couples find each other through an 'o-miai'. This involves an interview arranged by a go-between (a friend of the family) for the couple, often with the couple accompanied by both parents sitting round a table, refereed by the go-between.

After everyone has established what everyone's job and status is (very important), extremely polite and vague conversation ensues. Good question 'What is your hobby?' Good answer 'Music appreciation'. Bad question 'What's your favourite love hotel?' Bad answer 'My hobby's hang gliding'.

Couples who meet in the normal course of life and decide to take the plunge of their own accord exist, but still factors such as his social status and her family background, play a big part in the decision. It is vital to know that the Japanese for 'I want you to marry me' is 'Come and meet my parents next Sunday'.

There can be a lot of pressure to get married, especially on women. A girl approaching the age of 25 will get very nervous about being 'Christmas cake age'; just as you can't sell a Christmas cake on or after the 26th (not for what it's worth, anyway) so girls worry that they will be on the shelf if they don't get married in time. If you meet a single Japanese girl over 25 you should sympathise but be supportive and explain how in the West she would be regarded as laudably independent. Do not ask how many o-miais she has had.

Weddings take place at huge Wedding Halls and cost as much as several family cars. Any poster or advertisement with a picture of a woman in a black wig, red kimono and white hood you can confidently say is for a wedding hall.

There are two possible destinations for a honeymoon: Hawaii, and Guam.

Hawaii, being easier to pronounce in Japanese, and being half-full of half-Japanese anyway, is very popular. You can suggest that the ideal solution to the trade deficit the US runs with Japan would be to sell them Hawaii.

Love and Sex

Distinguish between this and marriage. Marriage is a business partnership whose purpose is to provide the man with a substitute mother, the mother with kids and money, and the kids with a family in Japan, and nothing to do with love or sex.

Make fine but unexplained distinctions between the two words for 'love', one being Japanese ('ai') and one being Japanese-English ('rabu', the nearest you can get to the word 'love' with Japanese sounds). Similarly between 'seiko' (as in the watch) and 'sekkusu', both of which mean 'sex' in Japanese. The English-derived words in each case have a rough, physical feel, rather than the abstract nature of the original Japanese words.

Japan has thousands of Love Hotels (in Japanese, 'Rabu Hoteru', you can say quite truthfully) across the country, where you can rent a room by the hour to do the necessary. Everything is done without ever seeing a face (disembodied hands collect the money and all doors are remote-controlled) to ensure maximum discretion.

You ought to claim to have been to a love hotel. Most are plain hotel rooms with a nice, big, bouncy bed, a few well-placed mirrors, a television with a 'mood video' supplied to get you in the right frame of mind, and a fridge packed with things like yogurt and KY Jelly. You can describe your consternation at not knowing which to eat because the writing on the cartons was in obscure Japanese.

Ambitious bluffers can describe more sophisticated versions of love hotels (they certainly exist) with water-beds, videos (to film yourself and watch the slow-motion replays), whips and chains, costumes, and so on. Love hotels come in all shapes and sizes (and so do the customers). Many are shaped like castles, some like temples, and you can even claim "to have been" to the one in Tokyo which is like the USS Enterprise complete with Star Trek costumes.

You give the appearance of one who really knows the country when you can confidently identify that window-less castle-shaped building just off the main road as a love hotel. The rooms have books to write your comments and suggestions in. Make sure they are extremely erotic.

Though the secretive nature of these establishments obviously encourages them as venues for businessmen seeing their secretaries, note that the biggest users are actually married couples. You can credit this to the average Japanese house having walls an eighth of an inch thick and the fact that Grandma, Grandad and the children are on either side. Saturday nights are booked solid, though if you go on a Monday afternoon, you can get unlimited time for a flat fee, and video yourself to your heart's content. This is the time you should claim to have gone.

Porn

Three facts summarise the Japanese attitude to pornography:

1. If you arrive at Narita airport and the customs man finds a copy of Playboy in your briefcase, he will confiscate it and lecture you about morality.
2. You can then walk outside and buy some hard core stuff from the ubiquitous vending machine outside.

3. A photo in a magazine can show anything however explicit except pubic hair, which is all covered or air-brushed out.

Sexism

Lament the amount of role-playing that goes on in Japanese society, even if you are a hard-line sexist.

If you are a man in Japan, you watch porn films, you earn the money, you go to hostess bars, you have sex outside marriage, and going into a kitchen is the worst thing that can happen. If you're a woman, you stay at home, push the kids through their education, spend the money, mother your husband, and not getting married is the worst thing that can happen.

The reason you should appear rabidly anti-sexist even if you aren't is that if you're a woman, you won't get poured drinks when out with a group of men, only orange juice; and, if you're a man and you're known to have once made yourself some toast or done any washing-up, you will be considered transsexual.

Many women work full-time hours for part-time pay in sweatshops with no holidays, no sick leave, and no rights. The rest are OL – office ladies, whose sole purpose is to make the tea and do photocopies. You can quite happily stick up for them, because everyone including the Japanese will agree what a scandal it is and then do nothing about it.

Contraception is a rarely mentioned business in Japan, so you can prove your familiarity with the society by knowing about it. The contraceptive pill is virtually impossible to get on prescription; the alternative is, unfortunately, the abortion clinic down the road. You can even claim to have heard of married couples using it as a form of contraception.

Manners

As everyone knows, the Japanese are the politest people in the world. You should know *how* they are polite though. They are polite to food and drink; they refer to rice as go-han (honourable rice), tea as o-cha (honourable tea) and toilets as o-toire (honourable toilets). Intimate parts of a woman's body are honourable too, but not a man's.

The Japanese very rarely speak directly; in business especially, but in life generally as well, they will erm and ahh and hesitate and leave things open rather than commit themselves to a decision. Therefore follow these rules when talking to them:

- if they say yes, they mean no
- if they say perhaps, they probably mean yes
- if they say no, they aren't Japanese.

The Japanese do not criticise each other, or anyone else, even in trying circumstances. If, for example, a Japanese arrives late for a social appointment (this happens all the time; the Japanese are rotten timekeepers outside of business and will often turn up to meet you at the station an hour or two late) no-one would say a word to the miscreant's profuse apologies. This is a good point to make as it implies you regularly meet with the Japanese.

Shop assistants are extremely polite but you should not say thank-you to them. The Japanese just ignore them.

It is often said that the politeness business is all about 'honne' and 'tatemae', the first being one's real thoughts, the second being what one says or how one behaves in public. For example, tatemae could be "We will give this plan our utmost consideration", honne "We think this is a load of rubbish". You should say this is overrated and point out that the same thing happens all the time in English ('We must have a drink together sometime', 'I'm afraid he can't speak to you, he's in a meeting, he'll call you back', 'I really want to keep you as a friend').

The Japanese all understand each other's hidden meanings perfectly whatever they appear to say. In fact, what they say to each other if they're anything but the closest of friends is limited to about twenty phrases anyway, so this is just as well. They can pick up minute clues to the speaker's real feelings from, for example, their expression, the tone of voice, the cut of their suit, or the probability of precipitation that day.

You have to remember that heaping one's own misery on someone else is extremely bad manners in Japan, hence the untroubled facade. A smile when they say 'our house has just been flooded' or 'my father died last night' shows their reluctance to burden you with their own problems, and not an incredible sense of humour.

So, if you see a Japanese:

a) crying and getting extremely emotional about something, you can be sure it's quite insignificant like losing a baseball match;

b) if you see a Japanese laughing, you'll know it's something disastrous for him or her, a death in the family perhaps;

c) if you see a completely passive, calm and polite Japanese, it probably means they're just about to take over your company.

Differences

It is often said that the Japanese 'think differently' from the rest of the world. This is based on a theory proposed by Tsunoda, a Japanese whose studies apparently showed that the Western brain is split into left-side-rational and right-side-emotional, while the Japanese mixes rational and emotional responses in the left side. What the Japanese do with the the right side of the brain is not said.

This, the theory continues, explains why the Japanese are less logical than Westerners. This logical Westerner vs. emotional Japanese idea is very strongly rooted, in fact the Japanese are explicitly taught it at school. It is very useful for:

- justifying things which are clearly wrong, such as there being no summer time;
- reinforcing 'nihonjinron', the idea the Japanese share with every other race in the world – that they themselves are somehow different, i.e. superior, to the rest of the world.

It's therefore a lot of fun to find as many counter-arguments to the 'non-logical' Japanese idea as possible, partly because only a connoisseur would challenge such as well-established idea, but mainly because it surprises the Japanese. For example:

a) the Japanese must be more logical than Westerners because they are the best mathematicians in the world

b) they write their names on Valentine cards, which is much more logical than trying to guess the sender as the emotional Westerner does

c) Japanese is much more logical than English. Japanese has a very simple word order and straightforward grammar. Try explaining the logic behind the English word order in 'I don't know what he does' instead of '. . . what does he'; or why the questions 'aren't you coming?' and 'are you coming?' expect the same answer; or rationalising the correct 'it's me' when the grammar predicts 'it is I'.

Koreans

The Koreans have some similarity with Indians and Pakistanis in Britain – immigrants from a former colony now discriminated against. In the Korean case most of them were brought by force from Korea as slave labour. It is worth knowing three interesting things about 'Koreans' born in Japan:

1. Even if you're born in Japan, you cannot be Japanese if your parents are not Japanese. This causes problems with third-generation 'Koreans' born in Japan of second-generation 'Korean' parents who turn out to be criminals. Japan tries to extradite them (because they're Korean) but Korea won't have them (because you can't actually extradite someone to a place they've never been). They also can't get any passports for either country.

2. Because of very large scale discrimination against Koreans by Japanese companies, they can only get employment being gangsters, pachinko hall owners and self-employed, and make millions.

3. They have to carry identity cards all the time.

You can talk confidently about the constitution which clearly forbids any discrimination – but only against Japanese citizens, and as the Koreans are not allowed Japanese citizenship they are exempt.

All foreigners are either Koreans, Blacks or Americans. Even the British are regarded as Americans. All foreigners have to carry an identity card which refers to the holder as 'THE ALIEN'.

The group never mentioned in Japan are the 'eta', or untouchables. Even a passing mention of the word, which means 'filth', is a good way to lose your company's account in Japan, permanently. The eta still exist, in certain areas on the edges of cities, do all the menial jobs, and until recently were not even counted as real people on the census.

Politics

Point out the similarities between Britain and Japan.

– Both are constitutional monarchies (except for Japan, which does not have a monarch but an emperor, and for Britain which does not have a constitution).

- Both are island countries (except for Japan which consists of several large islands, and for Britain which has three countries on one of its islands).
- Both have democratically elected Upper and Lower Houses (except for Japan which calls them Representatives and Councillors, and for Britain whose House of Lords is not elected).

Political trivia such as who is Prime Minister or which party is in power or how their system of proportional representation works need not concern you. All Japanese politicians tend to be very conservative.

Only the cognoscentus would know that in Japanese elections you are given a completely blank piece of paper as you enter the polling booth and merely write the name of the candidate of your choice. This poses obvious problems for illiterate, blind, armless or forgetful voters.

Japanese elections are notable for their strict interpretation of the rules concerning party political broadcasts. No aids are permitted at all – no visuals, graphics, diagrams – it's strictly a man talking to the TV camera or radio microphone about his policies for five minutes, and is therefore very dull.

In 1986 one of the candidates was deaf and dumb but, under the rules, was not allowed to have subtitles or a dubbed voice-over, 'to be fair to everyone else'. His television slot was therefore lost to anyone who couldn't understand sign language and his radio broadcast consisted of five minutes of unintelligible grunts.

Religion

There are some statistics you ought to remember about Japanese religion. They go a long way to avoiding having to answer the question 'What religion are the Japanese?'

- There are 220 million adherents of one religion or another
- 80 million Japanese do not profess to any religion at all
- The population of Japan is 120 million.

Don't attempt to draw any conclusions from these figures; just say that religion in Japan is approached very differently compared to the West (e.g. "There has never been a link in Japan between the Church and the State" which is hardly surprising as they had no churches until recently and have prefectures instead of states).

The 'religion' the Japanese practise at any given moment can change according to the circumstances:

a) festivals are Shinto
b) weddings are Shinto and/or Christian
c) funerals are Buddhist
d) day-to-day morals are based on the sayings of Confucius
e) other things are decided on how good for business they are.

It's always fun to tell apocryphal stories of converted, and hence baptised, Japanese acquaintances who introduce themselves to you "Hello, my name is Ichiroh Murakami, but my Christian name is George." There is a smallish but by no means negligible minority of Christians in Japan, with the most visible evidence of proselytising coming from the Mormon missionaries from America. They hunt in twos, going from door-to-door, talking very politely and unpushily in generally pretty good Japanese, for two years.

If you are feeling charitable, note that thanks to the efforts of these people there are now 1.4 million Christians in Japan. If you are feeling uncharitable, add that this is almost as high a percentage as there was in the 16th century.

SOCIALIZING

You will spend most of your evenings in Japan in bars. Do not be fooled into thinking that these are places to relax and enjoy yourself; most bars are just extensions of work and your behaviour will be closely watched. There are three types of places to drink after work:

1. **Pabbu**, 'pubs', which are easy to recognise because they are nothing like English pubs
2. **Sunakku**, 'snacks', which do not serve edible food;
3. **Baa**, 'bars', which serve a very limited selection of drinks, usually just whisky.

There are only four brands of beer in Japan. They are all exactly the same – light and fizzy, tasting something like unsweetened Lucozade, but won't aid recovery from anything except constipation. They are Kirin, Asahi, Sapporo and Suntory. The Japanese all have their firm favourites and stick to them (Kirin is often claimed to be best) so pick one and refuse to touch anything else. A great show is made of ordinary versus 'nama' beer, a token real ale which is translated as 'live beer'. Choosing nama beer is good for your image, even though it tastes exactly the same as normal beer and wouldn't show any signs of life even if you jump-started it.

Glasses in Japan should always be kept full, so keep your hosts well charged (they certainly will be when the bill comes, but don't worry: they'll pay). The amount of head on a beer is taken as a measure of how good it is, so never pour it out for others from a height of less than five feet. Japanese are always fascinated when you tell them that real ale in England has no head.

Japanese men all smoke. Japanese cigarettes:
a) are available from vending machines everywhere
b) are advertised on television and also by local councils who encourage people to smoke to raise taxes
c) have names like 'Peace' and 'Hope'.

51

Karaoke

You will not be able to avoid karaoke while you are in Japan. It is a peculiar concept whereby drunken people in bars get up on stage and sing the words of well known songs to a musical backing on tape, often accompanied by videos. Most of the songs are, of course, Japanese, and all sound exactly the same, so there's no point trying to remember any.

A good thing to say is "Ah, is this enka?" when someone is singing. Enka is a sentimental type of ballad, sometimes called 'Japanese blues' only inasmuch as it depresses everyone listening and is also best sung out of tune. This gives you the appearance of a music connoisseur, when in fact 99 per cent of slow songs sung in karaoke are enka so it's a fair bet.

You'll certainly be asked to sing. Refusal offends but acceptance ensures your popularity, and don't worry about your ability; the worse you sing, the better its reception . First, ask for the 'menu' – the list of songs. At the back will be the selection of foreign songs, and by an amazing coincidence these will be:

- *I Left My Heart In San Francisco*
- *Love Me Tender*
- *Bridge Over Troubled Water*
- *Yesterday*
- *My Way*.

Learn the words and the tune to some of these, claim they are your favourite songs in the world, and your free drinks for any night are assured. Always leave *My Way* for your encore.

As you will be taken out on average five times a week to karaoke bars in Japan, it can quickly get tedious singing the same songs. Suggested tactics to keep yourself sane are:

1. Sing the song in a heavy Japanese accent ('Ai rehuto mai haato in san huranshisuko'). It's fun but few people will notice.
2. Watch the video accompanying the song, which will probably be pornographic (*Yesterday* is often interesting) and exploit the phallic symbolism of the microphone.
3. Sing any words you like to the tune. It's amazing what can be done with *Love Me Tender*. Again, fun, but not many people will notice.

Food

Food in Japan is:
a) fishy, lean and still moving,
b) meaty, fatty and never moved in its life, or
c) pizza

Most of class (a) is 'Japanese food'. Japanese cuisine is some of the most attractively presented and skilfully put together in the world. Much of it is based on freshly caught raw fish, highly polished white rice, and unusual pickled vegetables. You can avoid it quite easily.

If your Japanese hosts point to something on the menu and ask 'Do you know sashimi?' or 'Do you know sushi?' they aren't asking about a person, but about a dish. Japanese menus are not nearly so complicated as they look, so just say "That's a kind of raw fish isn't it?", and you can never be far wrong.

Meat, like most of the Western businessmen in Japan, is well presented and costs around fifty pounds an hour; but is tasteless and fat. The most expensive comes from cattle ranches around Kobe where the cattle are kept in cramped artificial conditions all their lives and are force-fed large quantities of beer, like most Japanese businessmen in Japan.

Pizza therefore is the logical choice, except that it

invariably contains either meat or fish.

Always use chopsticks when you eat, even if it is pizza. The Japanese are convinced that foreigners cannot use chopsticks and will look amazed and invite their friends from down the road to watch you when you start to wield them. This is not sarcasm; though the Japanese do have sarcasm, they don't waste it on foreigners and will take whatever you say at face value. Practice at home with peanuts.

Insist that everyone in the West uses chopsticks "because there are many Chinese restaurants". That way if they query your method of holding them you can say it's the Chinese/Hong Kong/Thai style. You can justify anything with this so long as you don't spear your food with your chopsticks, which will get everyone in the place smiling at you; this means you have done the most offensive and tasteless thing imaginable and they wish you'd go home.

When you do get to eat raw fish, your hosts will probably order a variety of different types of fish and, as you eat, ask you what the name of each one is in English. You can say anything and they'll just say hohhh, hahhh, naruhodo, and words like that, and forget them the next morning. If the only fish you know are cod and haddock don't let on – it looks very bad. The Japanese are very good at knowing names of their fish, birds, trees and flowers, and you must be seen to do the same for your own food and flora. Use therefore any of these replies to 'How do you say in English this fish?' -

a)   horse mackerel
b)   deep sea bream
c)   blowfish
d)   lumpfish
e)   it's half dog salmon and half X-rayfish.

Use a similar approach when asked the name of trees and flowers. Compile lists of likely answers for yourself.

The two things to avoid on the menu are natto and odori-ebi. Natto is a sickly brown substance that looks and smells like rotten beans, which is probably because it is rotten beans. If challenged to eat it outbluff your challengers by saying you'll have some if they have some. Although claimed to be a 'delicacy' nobody with any brains eats it, and the Japanese are probably the brainiest race in the world. They will turn down your kind offer and your reputation and stomach will both remain intact.

Odori-ebi means 'dancing prawns' and are prawns so recently beheaded (alive) they are still moving. The head will be fried and brought to you after you've eaten the body. If your hosts insist on you trying some and you don't think you can manage it, your best recourse is probably to say it's very bad luck in the West to eat moving fish. The Japanese are very superstitious and might just sympathise. To counter all this you can tell them about delicious Western delicacies such as black pudding and jellied eels and tripe.

The bluffer is always sceptical of the ubiquitous exotic spice called 'aji-no-moto'. It is nothing more and nothing less than monosodium glutamate.

The surprising thing about Japanese food is how good it tastes once you get over the idea of eating rice, seaweed and raw egg for breakfast in your hotel (only in the cheapest downtown motels would you get a continental breakfast). Or at least that's what you should say.

Always do your bit for international understanding and at least try the food on offer; it pleases people enormously, and if you chew them really well, there is only a small likelihood of the prawn reconstituting in your stomach.

Names

When meeting a Japanese, you will exchange cards. You should have a business card, even if you're not in business, and if you do have one it will have the English on one side and the Japanese on the other. Always give the English side up first, so your acquaintance can pretend they can read English.

The purpose of cards for the Japanese themselves is so that they can establish what social status the other person has (they aren't able to tell from the outward appearance, of course, as they all wear identical suits) and hence know how deeply to bow, what form of polite language to use, etc. It is also handy for finding out how to write their new acquaintance's name in characters; the only other way of explaining which characters make up your name is to draw them invisibly on your hand, which causes all sorts of problems on the phone.

The Japanese identify strongly with their names so you should know something about them. Names were illegal in the Shogun period except for people who really needed them, like Samurai. Thus people were referred to as 'the fisherman who lives on the hill's third daughter' and so on. Then in the course of Westernisation around the 1860s they were made compulsory within a few years. In the struggle to get names for themselves everyone, with characteristic Japanese pragmatism, called themselves the first thing they saw that morning. This enables you to explain why there are only five or six surnames in Japan, such as 'Honda' (rice field) 'Ohta' (rice field again) 'Yamada' (rice field on a mountain), 'Tanaka' (another rice field).

All girls' names used to end in '-ko' (Tomoko, Toshiko, Yohko) but now the trend seems away from this, towards endings like '-mi' (Toshimi, Tomomi). Men's names are more imaginative though you still get points for recognising Ichiro as meaning 'first son', Jiro as 'second son', Saburo as 'third son' etc. A good talking point is that the Emperor, Hirohito, has no family name which must cause problems with driving licences.

56

THE LANGUAGE

Spoken Language

The Japanese language is often touted as having certain unique features, supposedly reflecting the uniqueness of the Japanese way of thinking. Deny them vigorously, as follows:

1. Japanese word order is unique in being backwards (No it isn't; Hindi, for example, has a similar word order, and you can't sweep 700 million Indians under the carpet.)
2. Japanese has a unique system of honorific language (Korean has more levels of honorifics, and there are fifty-five million of them, the Koreans that is.)
3. Japanese has words of one vowel sound (so does English, as in the word Aaaaaaaaaaaaaaaaa meaning 'You've just dropped the piano on my foot'.

Local dialects in Japan are called 'ben' – Tokyo-ben, Osaka-ben and so on. This is always a good talking point; when you find out someone comes from Ehime, say, ask if they speak Ehime-ben. Laughter is guaranteed. The great thing about ben is that you can blame your failure to understand somebody's Japanese on the fact that they are speaking 'inaka-ben' or 'country dialect'.

As in all countries the Japanese think they are the only country to have dialects so stress the more incomprehensible ones in England, for example flobbobnibob flobdob nibob lobob, an example of Billand-Ben.

Insist that spoken Japanese is, despite what you may have been told, very easy. This is because in order to save face and avoid uncomfortable differences of opinion, the Japanese go for maximum vagueness by only using five phrases most of the time. Sprinkle your conversation with them and you'll amaze all with your fluency. You can build whole conversations using only these five sentences:

a) Soh des' neh . . .

Means 'yes, that's right', though it also means 'that's a good question' (The correct reply to 'What is your final offer on this deal?' is 'Soh des' neh . . .'). The great thing about this is that it's always a safe answer to any question; Japanese can go for hours saying nothing but soh des' neh to each other.

b) Muzukashii des' neh . . .

Means 'yes, it's difficult' or 'mm, difficult to say', but remember that everything in Japan is difficult. Marriage is difficult. Learning English is difficult. Being abroad is difficult. Making a decision is difficult. (A variant on this is 'sorewa mondai des' neh . . .', 'yes, that's a problem'.)

c) Nan tte yuu no?

Means 'what's the Japanese for..?' or 'what's the word I'm looking for?'. A good delaying tactic, as it implies that:

i)   you know the word really but have temporarily forgotten it

ii) you already have several words in mind but none of them capture the subtle nuance you wish to express.

It often gets the message across anyway, without you committing yourself. Hence the Japanese use this phrase all the time.

d) . . . deske(re)do(mo)

Means '. . . but.' In Japanese it is very polite to end a sentence with 'but', although as word order in a Japanese sentence is backwards you can argue that it actually starts it. It softens the tone of a statement which might be misconstrued as provocative or tendentious; you say, for example, "This deal looks a little risky, but" or "I'm going to be a bit late for the meeting, but" or "It's raining today, but". Again, it implies you have a lot more to say about the matter, but are treating your unspoken views as understood by the listener, when in reality you may not want to risk saying anything else, but.

e) Wakarimash'ta
'Oh, I see' or 'Got it!'. Dismiss anyone who says it means 'understand' – it really means 'no further explanations are necessary' and is a good way of telling someone politely that you consider this part of the conversation closed.

Swear Words

There are no swear words in Japanese. It is too refined a language. This causes many problems in translating American cop shows, with consequent oddities like the exclamation 'shit!' being translated as 'yappari', which means 'nevertheless'.

Written Language

Rather like a film by famous Japanese director Akira Kurosawa, there are thousands of characters and you keep forgetting which is which and whether they're important. These characters ('kanji') were adopted from China. There are fifty thousand of them, and the only way to learn them is by writing them all out a hundred times a day, each.

Clearly fifty thousand is far too much to expect people to remember, so the figure has been cut down, and only three thousand or so are necessary to read an average book or magazine.

Unfortunately the Chinese teachers came from several different parts of the mainland so the pronunciation is inconsistent and unpredictable. In addition, the Japanese like to be creative and often just use an unexpected pronunciation for a kanji, particularly on names. It would, you say, be like spelling the place name 'Bath' as 'S-h-o-w-e-r' on the grounds that they mean almost the same.

To complicate things, each has an extra Japanese pronunciation, plus a few extra Japanese and Chinese pronunciations for good measure. The only way of knowing which is used when is to learn them all.

In addition there are two Japanese alphabets called 'the fifty sounds', so called because there are forty five of them. You can in theory write Japanese with these phonetic alphabets but the Japanese say this would be far too complicated. Written Japanese is therefore a mixture of Chinese characters, two Japanese alphabets and the odd bit of English.

The upshot is that no-one can read a newspaper completely right, few people can 'spell' more than a few well-known town and county names correctly, and even educated Japanese can only make a vague guess at how to read personal names.

Counters

This is by far the most interesting feature of the Japanese language, and therefore of the Japanese mind. They use different sets of numbers to count different types of object. They have one lot of numbers for counting big animals, another, quite different set, for counting flat objects, etc., ("just as in English we talk about 'two head of cattle', or 'five slices of toast'", you say). They got the idea from the Chinese but made it more complicated. You can have earnest conversations with Japanese asking for the correct way to count chopsticks or rabbits or airport runways.

The Japanese view of the world, then, classifies all objects into groups as follows, each having a different set of numbers to count them by. Make far-reaching inferences about the Japanese mind from this. Blame or explain anything you like on it.

People;
Small animals and fish, not including rabbits;
Large animals;
Birds (including rabbits);
Long narrow things;
Tiny things;
Flat things, not including tennis courts, airport runways or ponds;
Tennis courts, airport runways and ponds;
Machines;
Small ships;
Large ships;
Planes;
Hand tools, instruments and guns;
Books;
Newspapers;
Large buildings but not houses;
Houses but not housing lots;
Events and housing lots;
Bundles of spinach;
Bunches of other things but not spinach;
Sliced things;
Cups, without saucers;
Plates;
Suits and dresses;
Pairs of shoes;
Packs of cards and sets of tableware including cups and saucers together;
Chopsticks;
Things which do not fall into the above categories such as words, eggs and pieces of furniture.

This is how the Japanese mind classifies the world. It is the last word on Japan.

THE AUTHOR

Rob Ainsley was born in the 35th year of Showa in Hull, a difficult place for Japanese speakers to pronounce as neither the 'h', 'u' or 'l' sounds occur in their language. He went to Japan by mistake in 1984 and did not leave until two years later when he at last knew enough Japanese to ask for an airline ticket home.

He did several interesting things in Japan (none of them printable) and a few printable things (none of them interesting). Most of the time he lived in Okazaki, where everyone remembers him. This is probably why he dare not return there.

He learnt fluent Japanese by talking to hostesses in clubs. Nobody told him until it was too late that women's Japanese and men's Japanese is totally different and that he spoke like a woman. He did get offered several interesting jobs though. He re-learnt men's language by talking to businessmen in bars and now when speaking Japanese he sounds permanently drunk.

He works as a kind of magazine editor, sort of lives in Bath and is more or less single.

THE BLUFFER'S GUIDES

Available @ £1.00 each:

Accountancy	Marketing
Bluffing	Paris
Class	Philosophy
Consultancy	Photography
Feminism	Publishing
Hi-Fi	Sex
Hollywood	Teaching
Jazz	Television
Literature	Theatre
	Wine

Available @ £1.95 each:

Antiques	Japan
Ballet	Journalism
Cricket	Management
Computers	Maths
The EEC	Music
Fortune Telling	The Occult
Golf	University

All these books are available at your local bookshop or newsagent, or can be ordered direct from the publisher. Just tick the titles you require and fill in the form below. Prices and availability subject to change without notice.

Ravette Books Limited, 3 Glenside Estate, Star Road, Partridge Green, Horsham, West Sussex RH13 8RA

Please send a cheque or postal order, and allow the following for postage and packing. UK 25p for one book and 10p for each additional book ordered.

Name ....

Address ....

....

THE BLUFFER'S GUIDES

Planned or in preparation:

Architecture
Bank Managers
Beliefs
The Classics
Defence
Espionage
Finance
Gambling
High Society
Law
Millionaires
Opera
Politics
Property
Psychology
Public Speaking
Public Relations
Secret Societies

Selling
Ski-ing
Stocks & Shares
Travel
World Affairs

The Americans
The Australians
The British
The French
The Germans

Amsterdam
Berlin
Hong Kong
Moscow
New York